# LONDON'S RAILWAY TERMINI

## PHOTOGRAPHS AT THE END OF THE LINE

ISBN 978 1 85414 462 1

Published by
Capital History
www.capitalhistory.co.uk

Printed by Parksons Graphics

# LONDON'S RAILWAY TERMINI
## PHOTOGRAPHS AT THE END OF THE LINE

**KEVIN NIXON & PETER LLOYD**

CAPITAL HISTORY

# INTRODUCTION

This book is a photographic celebration of the remaining railway termini of London: those stations literally at the end of the line. Simon Jenkins stated in his 2017 celebration of *Britain's 100 Best Railway Stations* that: "I see the station …. not just as a building but as a social phenomenon, a place where people perform the timeless rituals, not just of travelling but of congregating, working, playing, greeting and parting".

In this he echoes the French poet Theophile Gautier (1811-1872) who, writing in a time of political upheaval and technological transformation, stated that the almost phantasmagorical new railway buildings springing up all over Europe were the "… cathedrals of the new humanity … the meeting points of the nations, the centre where everything converges". "Cathedrals of the new humanity" is an inspiring phrase, one that suggests both a faith in technological advance and an optimistic view of human potential, but I wonder if railway stations will become, or maybe already are, "museums of an old order"? Perhaps we should treat them as such, as national monuments and free of the need to 'monetise' every square inch. Use them, of course, as functional buildings but also celebrate them as objects of beauty.

Gautier's phrase "the new humanity" highlights the immense social, industrial, commercial, political and artistic shifts that occurred in his lifetime. Eric Hobsbawm's works, *The Age of Revolution* (1789-1848) and *The Age of Capital* (1848-1875) take 1848, the so-called 'year of revolutions', as the fulcrum of these two 'Ages', when revolutionary political ideas co-existed with revolutionary technical advances. By then the first of the great stations had already opened in London, Paris and Berlin and the sense of potential societal transformation would have been palpable. Railways opened up, not just England but – often using British engineers – whole continents.

The original 'cathedrals of steam' were the result of genius, vision, determination and skill (as well as megalomaniacal levels of ego, hubris, self-aggrandisement and ruthlessness, not to mention speculative frenzy and dishonesty). The engineers of the Victorian trainsheds were the first hi-tech architects – anticipating the Fosters, Rogers and Grimshaws of the present day by a hundred years – pushing building technology into barely imaginable great leaps forward.

From the Rainhill Trials of 1829, won by the Stephensons' *Rocket* steam locomotive, which were the starting gun for the race to passenger rail, it was only one year to the inauguration of the world's first passenger train line, the Liverpool to Manchester, in 1830. A flurry of building followed and all of London's rail termini, with one exception, were built within a 40-year period, from the first London Bridge station in 1836 through to the original Liverpool Street in 1874, with only Marylebone coming later in 1899.

While the achievements were extraordinary – and often magnificent – little attention was paid to the human cost: tens of thousands of houses were demolished to make way for the rail tracks and stations and many more thousands of people were dispossessed and made homeless. Even more shamefully the 'railway mania' was given the financial boost it needed in no small part by the ending of slavery.

The cities of London, Bristol, Liverpool, Manchester and Glasgow had long prospered because of the trade in enslaved people and in the cotton, sugar and tobacco they were forced to grow, and it was this prosperity that made the coming rail network feasible, but The Slavery Abolition Act of 1833 which formally abolished slavery within the British Empire (with significant exceptions) also made provision for "… compensating the Persons hitherto entitled to the Services of such Slaves". The Legacies of British Slave-ownership Centre, set up by University College London, states that the Act granted "£20 million in compensation, to be paid by British taxpayers to the former slave-owners". A total of 46,000 individual claimants were paid the modern equivalent of £17 billion (although that sum is widely questioned with estimates ranging from £20 billion to £100 billion). The government loan taken out to fund the compensation was only fully repaid in 2015, 182 years later.

The LBS Centre has carried out an immensely detailed study of which slave owners profited from the loss of their 'assets' (the enslaved humans) and where that money went – and a great deal went into the burgeoning railway boom.

The injection of this cash into railway stocks (an early example of money laundering) had predictable results. Hundreds of miles of track were built, many hundreds more approved and people from almost every social stratum rushed to invest in the first great railway boom. And then it went bust. This inevitable 'market correction' in 1837 might have ruined many people but it did not kill the railways: the seeds had been sown. Engineers, architects and builders had seen the light, as had the following shoal of entrepreneurs, speculators and wide boys. The bursting bubble of 1837 coincided with Queen Victoria's accession to the throne and the Victorian Age, when Britain became the industrial powerhouse of the world, was born. It was a crucible of invention that unleashed previously unimagined talent and, for all its inequities, allowed some people from simple, working families to flourish.

The forerunners of them all were George and Robert Stephenson but Isambard Kingdom Brunel is often cited as the personification of the spirit of the age, and understandably so given his achievements – The Great Western Railway, the SS *Great Britain*, Paddington station, numerous bridges and tunnels and on and on. He, his father, Marc, and son, Henry Marc, were all engineers. The extended Cubitt family produced engineers and builders who shaped London; there were many notable architects in the Wyatt family; the names Hawkshaw, Hood and Fowler all left notable achievements but someone less readily associated with railways played a seminal role in the design of the railway trainshed, the constructions that rivalled cathedrals and became emblematic of the age.

Joseph Paxton (1803-1865) was the seventh son of a farming family who started his employment at Chatsworth House in Derbyshire, the home of the dukes of Devonshire, as a garden boy and died as Sir Joseph Paxton, horticulturist, architect, visionary thinker and railway pioneer. Over his lifetime he designed numerous parks and gardens, a municipal cemetery,

Mentmore and the Chateau de Ferrieres for different branches of the Rothschild family, became an MP, made money from his directorships of various rail companies, but continued to work as Chatsworth's head gardener where, together with Decimus Burton, he designed and built the Great Conservatory. Completed in 1840 this glasshouse was a leviathan – 227 feet long and 123 feet wide – and revolutionary in structure: the enormous area was spanned by arches of laminated wood, supported by cast iron beams and columns and glazed with sheets of glass bigger than had ever been produced before.

When Paxton became a director of the Midland Railway, John Ellis, the Chairman of the company, encouraged Paxton to develop his ideas for a glass display hall for the Great Exhibition of 1851. It was to be even larger than Chatsworth's building, a staggering 1848 feet long by 454 feet wide; 770,00 square feet (nearly 18 acres) but designed to be built in modular form which made it significantly less expensive than the many other competing designs.

The selection committee that accepted Paxton's design for the Exhibition Hall included railway pioneers Robert Stephenson, Isambard Kingdom Brunel and William Cubitt and it is possible to trace the inspiration for many of the great train sheds, the cathedrals of steam, directly back to Paxton's conservatory at Chatsworth via the Great Exhibition Hall. So popular was the Great Hall that it became known as The Crystal Palace and at the end of the Exhibition it was disassembled and rebuilt at a site in Sydenham as a tourist attraction. Fittingly, a dedicated railway line was set up to take people from a station in Battersea to view it.

Eric Hobsbawm notes, with some admiration, in *The Age of Capital*, "The combination of romanticism, enterprise and finance...." that the building of the railways represented. He was, however, very well aware that, like any boom, the railways drew scoundrels to them. One of his examples is the "economic conquistador" Henry Meiggs (1811-77), an American who was forced to flee San Francisco to avoid the consequences of various frauds but became a prolific railroad builder in South America. He was, says Hobsbawm, "by any standards a dishonest adventurer... (but) .... can

anyone who has seen the Peruvian Central Railway deny the grandeur of the concept and achievement of his romantic if rascally imagination?".

Railways, and the driving forces behind them, elicit powerful and contradictory reactions. Beauty out of brutality always will.

Boom and bust were the rhythm of railway expansion and fortunes were made and lost, casual investors were ruined, some became rich, and an un-coordinated web of track was laid, often with competing companies running side by side, scrabbling to bring their lines into the most advantageous sites in London.

In our London-centric age there may be a tendency to think that the London termini were created as origin points serving routes that allowed Londoners to venture from the capital, whereas the various rail lines came from the great northern industrial cities of Birmingham, Derby, Sheffield, Manchester, Liverpool, Leeds and the port city of Bristol, and brought with them the produce that London needed: coal, bricks, iron, steel and foodstuffs – famously beer into St Pancras from Burton-upon-Trent and milk into Paddington.

Gaining a foothold in the capital, however, wasn't easily done. North of the Thames, canny dynasties like the Grosvenors and Russells understood the value of their property holdings in areas such as Belgravia, Mayfair and Bloomsbury and would not be railroaded (a phrase believed to be American in origin) into selling their prime central London real estate for short-term gain. Victoria station was eventually allowed into the Westminster estate but other stations had to settle for sites on the periphery of the 19th century city. South of the river the huge land interests of various bishoprics (London, Winchester and Rochester) were more willing to allow the railways closer to the centre, with London Bridge and the original Waterloo Junction almost touching the banks of the Thames.

The map of rail termini in London reads like a diagrammatic representation of invading armies encircling an enemy: columns of invaders advancing upon the city from all points of the compass only to be halted at the outskirts. This fact did not stop Euston from erecting what can only be described as a triumphal arch (built in 1837, but demolished in 1962).

Competition between rail companies and immovable landlords deprived London, for better and for worse, of having a grand central station, as epitomised by the German *Zentralbahnhof* or *Hauptbahnhof* and the American Union Station (most magnificently in New York). Gradually, the Underground system linked the termini: initially the Metropolitan Railway – the world's first underground railway, which opened in 1863 – connected Paddington, Euston and King's Cross, and plans were soon made with the District Railway to extend the line into a circle. However, competition with the District delayed the process and the route was only completed after government intervention in 1884, with District trains running clockwise and Metropolitan trains running anticlockwise around the loop. Although all the termini are served by the now-integrated Underground, some still remain slightly adrift and for the through-traveller London is still a time-consuming and often difficult pinch point.

The great provincial cities fed the growing beast of London until the beast consumed them. The relative decline of each of these cities was matched by the growth of London, and the eventual destruction of heavy industry in the 20th century marked their absolute decline while the Thatcher years and the financialisation of the economy confirmed London's dominance.

Each rail company marked its arrival in London not only with magnificently engineered trainsheds but also with grand hotels built in a mishmash of familiar architectural styles (sadly none of them embracing the industrial aesthetic of the sheds) leaving the trainsheds hidden behind unthreatening, stage-set buildings that acted as camouflage for the revolutionary structures behind them. The notable exception is King's Cross, where the hotel was set to one side to allow the undisguised expression of the arched platform canopies in the station frontage. St Pancras hotel is probably the most notable of these hotels today because of its relatively recent rescue from the wrecker's ball and its glorious restoration but in their day Marylebone, Liverpool Street, Charing Cross and Victoria all cut quite a dash; any of them would have made fabulous locations for various affairs of the heart, all the way from tentative rendezvous, romantic trysts and nuptial celebrations to more or less tawdry assignations.

In the same way that boom inevitably follows bust, the areas proximate to railway hotels may bask in the reflected glory of money and sophistication for a while but, with seeming inevitably, cheap boarding houses, poverty, beer, and brothels encroach and eventually overwhelm. The King's Cross area was notorious throughout the 1970s and 80s for street prostitutes, kerb-crawling and solicitation, coinciding with the neglect and near abandonment of St Pancras. Much of Camden was razed to accommodate Euston station and it, too, acquired a reputation for destitution and down-at-heel accommodations. Walter Sickert, one of the Edwardian painters of the Camden Town Group, showed mundane, dark, despondent, disquieting and often threatening images, not least *Jack the Ripper's Bedroom* (1907) and *The Camden Town Murder* (1908).

Earlier painters dealt directly with the new steam age. Britain's most revolutionary painter, J.M.W. Turner, was equivocal about it: *The Fighting Temeraire* (1839) was a mournful depiction of the victory of steam over sail, while *Rain, Steam and Speed* (1844) was a thrilling, but also frightening, evocation of the results of that victory and the coming of the railways. The architect and accomplished artist Thomas Talbot Bury documented the earliest days of rail, notably the heroic excavations, viaducts and bridges of the infrastructure for the Liverpool and Manchester Railway that he worked on. The French Impressionists embraced the railway age: Claude Monet painted the *Gare Saint Lazare* (1877) and the railway bridge at Argenteuil a number of times as well as making no fewer than 37 paintings of Charing Cross railway bridge between 1899 and 1905. The Fauve Andre Derain created his own, explosively colourful, view of Charing Cross bridge in 1906.

The most established of Establishment artists in Britain at the time, William Powell Frith, painted *The Railway Station* in 1862, perhaps still the best example of the communality of train travel, where wealth and ruin coexist (and where the ornate ironwork of Paddington can be clearly seen) while his later series of paintings, The Race for Wealth, illustrated the rise and fall of an unscrupulous financial speculator – one, surely, who gambled on the railway boom – neatly bookending the story of the early railways.

The amalgamation of railway companies that had begun in the 19th century continued into the early 20th century until the First World War forced government control onto the network. Rather than outright nationalisation after the war, however, and despite the advantages demonstrated during the war, monolithic control was resisted and individual companies reclaimed their routes. By 1923 this was no longer practicable and further amalgamation was forced on the system. The so-called 'Grouping' rationalised ownership into the Big Four: the Great Western Railway, the London and North Eastern Railway, the London, Midland and Scottish Railway and the Southern Railway. These survived until 1947 when the entire system was finally nationalised and British Rail emerged. BR acquired a reputation for inefficiency, poor labour relations and underinvestment creating a death-spiral that was only ended when BR was privatised, beginning in 1994, with services being run on a franchise basis by independent companies (some of them controlled by the national rail services of a number of European companies) while infrastructure became the responsibility of firstly Railtrack and then Network Rail. Passenger numbers increased steadily and services improved but so did fares, and the largely hidden government subsidies are huge, some estimates putting these at up to three times the pre-privatisation level. The collapse of rail travel due to Covid-19 meant greater government input and the British railway network and its model of ownership will probably have to be reassessed once more.

Recent history has seen a number of admirable renovation projects that have gone some way to make up for the unwise air-rights developments over some of London's termini that the property boom of the 1980s encouraged. In fact, in many ways, the past twenty years have been a golden age for at least some of London's termini. Paddington, St Pancras, King's Cross and Liverpool Street have been restored to a former glory, while London Bridge and Blackfriars have been wholly changed and for the better. The Victorian age witnessed a particularly flamboyant flowering of individual talent, but the architectural and engineering practices of today have achieved similar feats.

# BLACKFRIARS

Blackfriars is, like London Bridge, a station that is both a terminus and a through station, half its four platforms being for terminating services. A station called Blackfriars was opened by the London Chatham & Dover Railway (LC&DR) company in 1864, but on the south bank of the River Thames, and a very substantial thing it was, too. Designed by Joseph Cubitt, this was one of the many Cubitt involvements in railway construction. It was, however, only ever going to be an intermediate station in the campaign to cross the Thames and establish a station (or two) in the City itself. Cubitt's equally monumental bridge followed shortly after.

A station on the present site, then named St Paul's, opened in 1886 and was only renamed Blackfriars in 1937. St Paul's station was described as small and cheaply built, no doubt because the LC&DR was cash-strapped by that time. No one mourns its passing but it's a shame Cubitt's long warehouse-like building on the south of the Thames did not survive. I think it could have been beautifully updated by today's architects. As it was, it was relegated to a supporting role, becoming a goods yard within five years of its opening and the home of a fortress-like building in the 1970s (since thankfully demolished). A major residential development is now built on it.

Blackfriars station was subject to major rebuilding in the 1970s, including offices above, and most recently in 2009–2012 but its street presence plays second fiddle today to the bridge. The bridge is the highlight; indeed it is the bridge that is the station. Cubitt's bridge was most notable for the immense piers and columns that supported the track deck. As originally built, it took four sets of rails over the river on a 933ft lattice girder structure using five spans. Each pier comprised a stone base with a cluster of four cast iron columns.

The rapidly increasing popularity of train travel made expansion necessary and one railway bridge soon became two, with a bigger bridge being built alongside Cubitt's by John Woolf Barry and Henry Mark Brunel in 1886. The first bridge was dismantled in 1985, leaving the red, iron pillars and their granite bases enigmatically still standing in the river alongside the newer bridge.

By 2009 a radical rebuild was called for and a £600 million project started. The upgrading of the station involved widening the bridge, making use of the Cubitt piers. Enough of the pillars remain independent, however, to stand in the river, acting, it is claimed, as navigation aids. I prefer to think of them as works of industrial art.

The architects Pascall+Watson were responsible for the original design concept. Consulting engineers Tony Gee together with Jacobs undertook the widening of the bridge and the redevelopment of the Network Rail and Underground stations. This was all part of the Thameslink Programme for increasing capacity on one of the fastest-growing passenger routes in London. In order to accommodate new and longer trains the entire length of the bridge was roofed over and the bridge becomes the platform area. 4,400 solar panels were incorporated into the roof design and now provide half of all the energy used by the station.

A second access point on Bankside creates (or, perhaps more accurately, re-creates) access from south of the river, providing a much needed station for Tate Modern and the Globe theatre – not to mention the many apartment and hotel developments in the area.

Internally, the covered bridge is aero engineering-modern with a ceiling of riveted aluminium 'wings' alternating with glazed panels which bring natural light in from above while the almost seamless glass walls provide matchless views of the river. Externally, the way the angled solar panels alternate with the glass fillets in the zig-zag roofline creates a profile with a pleasingly syncopated rhythm. Sunrise and sunset seen from the seat of a commuter train idling at the platform must be worth closing one's laptop for.

At night, from either bank, the illuminated platforms stretch a band of platinum light across the river. Once you've visited Blackfriars you wonder why the other bridge stations haven't made more of their locations.

While I don't love the frontage of Blackfriars station onto Queen Victoria Street, it is at least light, bright and airy and the architects made the most of the awkward site and reduced space that was left for them with which to work. The only remains of the original station are a wall of sandstone blocks, each engraved with the names of the destinations that were once served. These were saved and remade into what amounts to a work of art. They are a delightful mix of the exotic and the mundane and have been arranged in such a way that they read almost like a poem:

*Berlin Bickley Maidstone Frankfort*
*Bremen Bromley Ramsgate Lausanne*
*Dresden Faversham Walmer Wiesbaden*

They are the romance of train travel made manifest. Where shall I go today? I wonder how many people simply left their ordinary lives and the smog of Victorian London behind and boarded a train on a whim? It's worth visiting Blackfriars for this wall alone. Brighton seems to be the most exotic destination for today's runaways.

A beautifully restored LC&DR coat of arms is visible from the south-western corner of the bridge, but the best position to see it from is from is the Thames Path.

# CANNON STREET

Little survives of the original Cannon Street station, and what does – the two riverside towers that once supported a mighty arched roof – feels rather forlorn. A series of less-than-successful attempts to replace the railway hotel that once occupied the street frontage and half-hearted modernisations of the station created nothing of note until the most recent modifications.

Whether the new offices adequately honour the train station is debatable. The entrance to the station is elegant to the point of being self-effacing: if it was only an Underground station one might think it was refined, but as the way into a mainline station it is too modest. As in so many air rights developments, the need to maximise lettable space (without, in this case, rising too high in its sensitive City location) made compromise necessary.

The original hotel – the City Terminus Hotel, opened 1867 – was by Edward Middleton Barry, the same architect who designed the still-standing Charing Cross Hotel and was a 'high Victorian jumble of Italianate and Flemish Renaissance styles', according to Alan A Jackson, and, as such, I don't miss it. It was, however, considered rather special in its day and was immortalised by T.S. Eliot in The Waste Land, in which a Mr Eugenides asked his friend to 'luncheon at the Cannon Street Hotel'. Literary immortality could not guarantee physical immortality, however, and the hotel was knocked down and replaced in the post war years by what is described as a 'bland' office block by John Poulson, the famed architect/businessman/crook. It was in turn replaced in 2011 by the current building.

The street frontage is now a macho climbing frame of exposed girders and tensioning diagonals, while the side return facing Dowgate Hill is, rather confusingly, quite different. Massively over-scaled ellipses are, in fact, wishbone trusses and part of an ingenious exoskeleton. This transfers the load of the structure to ground bearing points, an engineering solution of which any of the architects of the great train sheds would be proud. This design allowed the station to operate throughout its construction and creates open floor space within. The way the building cantilevers over the main line and Underground stations isn't the only advantage: according to the architects, Foggo Associates, it minimises 'the impact on the Scheduled Ancient Monument of the Roman Governor's Palace below'. That work was completed in 2011.

Behind this, where the train shed once stood and abutting the Thames, is Cannon Bridge House. It has an award-winning roof garden with glorious views of the river but what it presents to the river is disappointing. The Wren-inspired towers still stand sentry on the river frontage today but why they would want to protect the structure between them is anybody's guess. Images of the earlier station show them supporting the almost semi-circular arch of the Hawkshaw and Barry shed of 1866, the different elements seemingly in perfect balance. A great dark maw below the arched roofline, lies ready to consume anything that strays into its vicinity. How the Victorians so quickly accepted these alien structures is extraordinary.

The shed was a mighty 700 feet long and almost as high as the 135 feet towers. Anything that came after was doomed to appear enervated in comparison but what is there now seems particularly uninspiring. Ironically, Historic England have offices in the building. The train shed was damaged by bombs during the war and was dismantled in 1957. The towers survived the bombing and their retention and repair was one of the Railway Heritage Trust's first successes.

Out of a £410 million budget for the redevelopment of Cannon Street, £20 million was set aside for improving the main line station (e-architect.com 18 January 2008) which may not have been enough. The platforms are claustrophobic with a low ceiling and bare functionality is their only claim. Electric trains have used the station since 1926.

It is the river that makes Cannon Street: boarding a train here can't be a totally dismal affair; being able to look out over the river, albeit briefly, must lift the spirits just a little. The bridge that serves the station is a strictly functional structure and all the better for it. Designed by John Hawkshaw, the 706ft long bridge was originally 80ft wide and carried five tracks. It was supported on four piers each with four columns, 18ft in diameter. The bridge opened in 1866, but by the mid-1880s needed to be widened to 120ft, two more columns being added to each pier to carry the larger deck.

These massive columns brook no nonsense, and it couldn't be described as anything but functional. At night its austere silhouette is really rather pretty when lit up. Together with all the bridges that cross the Thames in central London, from Tower Bridge to the Albert Bridge, it is part of the Illuminated River project, described as the longest art work in the world and funded by a number of charitable bodies led by The Rothschild Foundation.

The interior of the River Building was very nicely refurbished, with particular attention paid to the brickwork, by Stiff+Trevillion in 2017.

# CHARING CROSS

Charing Cross suffers from what is a familiar story: there was money to be made from exploiting the air-rights above stations, so why not squash the train shed and build something gargantuan on top? The Terry Farrell-designed behemoth is unarguably a commanding presence on the river. It has all the swaggering arrogance of the original 1864 structure, and is one of the most successful examples of Post Modernism in Britain. But there is still the lingering feeling of 'What if…?'

Should more importance have been given to the platforms and a much greater allowance made for headroom? Whatever Feng Shui is, these platforms don't have enough of the good stuff. My other 'what if' is, what if the hotel facing the Strand had been flattened at the same time as the shed? What if less importance had been given to 'heritage' and more to the theatre of travel? My feeling is that Farrell could have designed something that better married railway operational needs with the money-making potential of office and hotel developments.

Sir John Hawkshaw was one of the extraordinary breed of Victorian engineers, starting his career in his native Yorkshire. He became the chief engineer of the Manchester and Leeds Railway in 1845 and later worked internationally on both railway and canal projects. In 1863, his inquiry into the feasibility of the Suez Canal allowed construction to go ahead.

He was also responsible for bringing the South Eastern Railway to the Charing Cross site that had been occupied previously by the Hungerford produce market. In 1845 Brunel had built a suspension footbridge for access from the south bank. Demolition was needed for a new bridge to be built so that the railway could reach Charing Cross.

Hawkshaw's trussed iron railway bridge of 1864 was a considerable affair, with the nine spans supported on mammoth cast-iron cylinders and incorporating two of the original Brunel brick piers. To describe the design as 'industrial' is probably an understatement. By 1887, as demand increased, the bridge had to be widened and it now carries three fast line and two slow line tracks.

After spanning the river, trains arrived on the north bank in an elevated position. Hawkshaw designed a huge arched train shed, 164 ft wide with a single span wrought iron roof 102 ft high. It looked magnificent in an 1864 rendering of it in the *Illustrated London News*, but perhaps it was too magnificent. It collapsed in 1905. It was replaced with a more prosaic post and girder structure supporting a ridge and furrow roof – which is still in evidence in the concourse area.

The station was built on a brick-arched undercroft, which came to be used as wine cellarage. From street level on the Strand, the brick substructure is approximately 30 feet high at the level of the present-day Embankment. This was one of the major infrastructure projects of the day, designed to ease traffic congestion between the West End and the City and was built on land reclaimed from the Thames. It was completed in 1870, the creation of the eminent Victorian Joseph Bazalgette, most famous for the London sewerage and drainage system.

The pair of pedestrian bridges built by Lifschutz Davidson Sandilands for HM The Queen's Golden Jubilee opened in 2003. They now flank – and disguise – Hungerford Bridge. However, they have been a huge popular success and helped to revitalise the South Bank. They also provide some of the best views of London and it was an unforgivable mistake that they weren't part of the Farrell remit. (There is a constrained connection from station to bridge, but its use late at night is not recommended and it's not even pleasant by day).

The hotel was designed by Edward Middleton Barry (son of Sir Charles Barry) and is Grade II listed. The additional two floors that were not part of the original design look like an afterthought and don't help the composition of the façade, while the conservatories over the original cab archways were a later addition. They now look tired and shabby.

There is no grand entrance to the concourse; in fact there is barely adequate access for the number of travellers who now use the station from the small forecourt that abuts the Strand. Most of the arches have been colonised by shops, or – more understandably – the Underground entrance, toilets, ticketing and the hotel entrance. Imagine how much better the concourse would be if these rudimentary arches could be turned into a full cloister that completely opened the station to a pedestrianised square. At the moment it is the taxi drop-off area and the location of the under-appreciated Queen Eleanor Memorial Cross, designed by E M Barry and carved by the eminent architectural sculptor Thomas Earp in 1865. The structure is a free interpretation of a cross that had marked the final resting place of the body of Edward I's wife on its way to burial in Westminster Abbey in 1290.

Once you have entered the station, the simple glazed roof is pleasingly industrial and would suit a market hall perfectly. This is both a compliment and a criticism: its lack of grandiosity has charm, but Charing Cross is a major London station. Farrell's work of 1990 should have taken in the concourse and, at least, its interface with the hotel: today the concourse is too small, the Underground access is less than ideal, the retail outlets are too banal and the space is definitely looking tatty. If Network Rail ever has any spare money, it is time to rethink Charing Cross.

As it stands, the platforms right at the river end are uncomfortably narrow and their use has to be restricted for safety reasons. Yes, they could be extended further into the concourse at the Strand end, but that is tight enough already. Possible remedies would be to demolish the Grade II listed hotel or to widen Hungerford Bridge. But both would be exceedingly costly and might attract some considerable opposition.

# EUSTON

The London & Birmingham Railway (L&BR) announced its arrival in London in 1837 with admirable panache in the construction of a vast Doric arch. This was completed a year after the station opened. The Arch and accompanying paired lodges on either side were designed by Philip Hardwick, more notable nowadays for his work on Liverpool's Royal Albert Dock. It had no purpose other than to celebrate the L&BR. Hardwick, together with his son, Philip C. Hardwick, also designed the original Great Hall, by all accounts a splendid and luxurious affair. The arch was demolished in 1962, together with the equally flamboyant Great Hall, as part of the rebuilding of the station in the 1960s. This is an act that is still resented by many. If the brand new Euston goes ahead, I don't think many people will be sad to see the present building go.

Euston. I should love you. Modern and muscular, a hammer to traditionalism... oh, if only it had worked. It doesn't. Today the façade is a featureless motorway bridge of a building, all black now, with sightless windows, whereas, as originally planned, it was the acme of 1960s shopping precinct chic; glazed walls facing a pedestrian square, elegantly narrow concrete columns clad in granite and arranged as a rhythmic colonnade supporting the strong horizontal of the roof line with a clerestory above that. The square (it was probably called a 'plaza' in 1966) that fronts the station now seems grossly inadequate and has been clogged with the usual eating and drinking places and is ringed around with office buildings which should work better than they do. The concourse was designed to be a showcase of modern functionality: once considered large and spacious, with a floor of beautiful grey-green marble, an easily read information board and an easily accessed set of platforms, each long enough to cope with the longest of trains of the day, it must have been much admired. The floor is still impressive but rarely seen due to the sheer number of travellers, usually with bulky suitcase and a wayward sense of direction. The platforms are low ceilinged and oppressive and the narrow ramps that lead to them form a river-race of torrential humanity when the starting gun of departure time is announced.

The concourse built in the sixties was 30,000 sq feet, more than adequate for the projected number of travellers and almost entirely glazed, except for the north wall which housed the state of the art 'electro-mechanically operated train indicator' and was full of natural light. The Travel Centre could not be more futuristic and still stands up well, even today. Fifteen passenger platforms were built plus three for mail and parcel traffic; access to Underground services was incorporated; motor vehicles were separated from pedestrian routes and cars could be parked in a multi-storey below the concourse. Things started to go wrong in the 1970s when Richard Seifert, flamboyant millionaire architect of 600-odd buildings in London alone – most notably Centrepoint (1966) and Tower 42 (originally the NatWest Tower) (1991) – built the 'miserable range of polished, dark stone-clad offices' that now occupy much of the forecourt. Seifert's work is in the process of being re-evaluated but this has come too late for these buildings, which deserve to go (although under different circumstances I might be rooting for the low block that defines the southern edge of the square).

The heavy, concrete, ribbed ceilings are artfully lit and have a monumentality that deserves to be recorded if not saved. The station shares a birthday with the ultimate film of the Swinging Sixties, Blow Up, by Michelangelo Antonioni, and is contemporaneous with the mini skirt, the Mini car and the E-type Jaguar. If it is judged as a manifestation of the tectonic social shifts of the optimistic Swinging Sixties and of Harold Wilson's 'white heat of the technological revolution' it should not be judged too harshly.

If the visualisations of Grimshaw's new station are anywhere near the completed reality, with winged canopies over-sailing a light-filled, multi-levelled concourse and platform area, the station will rival any of the original termini for engineering audaciousness and ambition and be more than capable of elevating the spirit. If it is anywhere near as good as Grimshaw's Lubetkin Prize winning Southern Cross station in Melbourne, Australia, it will be well worth waiting for. It is scheduled to complete in 2033, with a much less flamboyant building, also by Grimshaw, to be built in Birmingham.

In case anyone seriously plans to rebuild the Euston Arch in front of the Grimshaw station, remember it was a great slab of unsophisticated stonework that even in its day was criticised for its hubris, not least by Augustus Welby Pugin, eminent proponent of the High Victorian Gothic style, who described the Arch as a 'Brobdingnagian absurdity' in *An Apology for the Revival of Christian Architecture*, 1843. Pugin also – inadvertently, surely, given his penchant for decorative flourishes – wrote the manifesto for every 'modernist' architect of every age in his critique: 'The architects have evidently considered it an opportunity for showing off what they could do instead of carrying out what was required' (Quoted in *London's Termini*, Alan A. Jackson 1985).

Like the supposedly iconic twin towers of Wembley Stadium, without which 'Wembley would not be Wembley' according to many, the Arch is best forgotten.

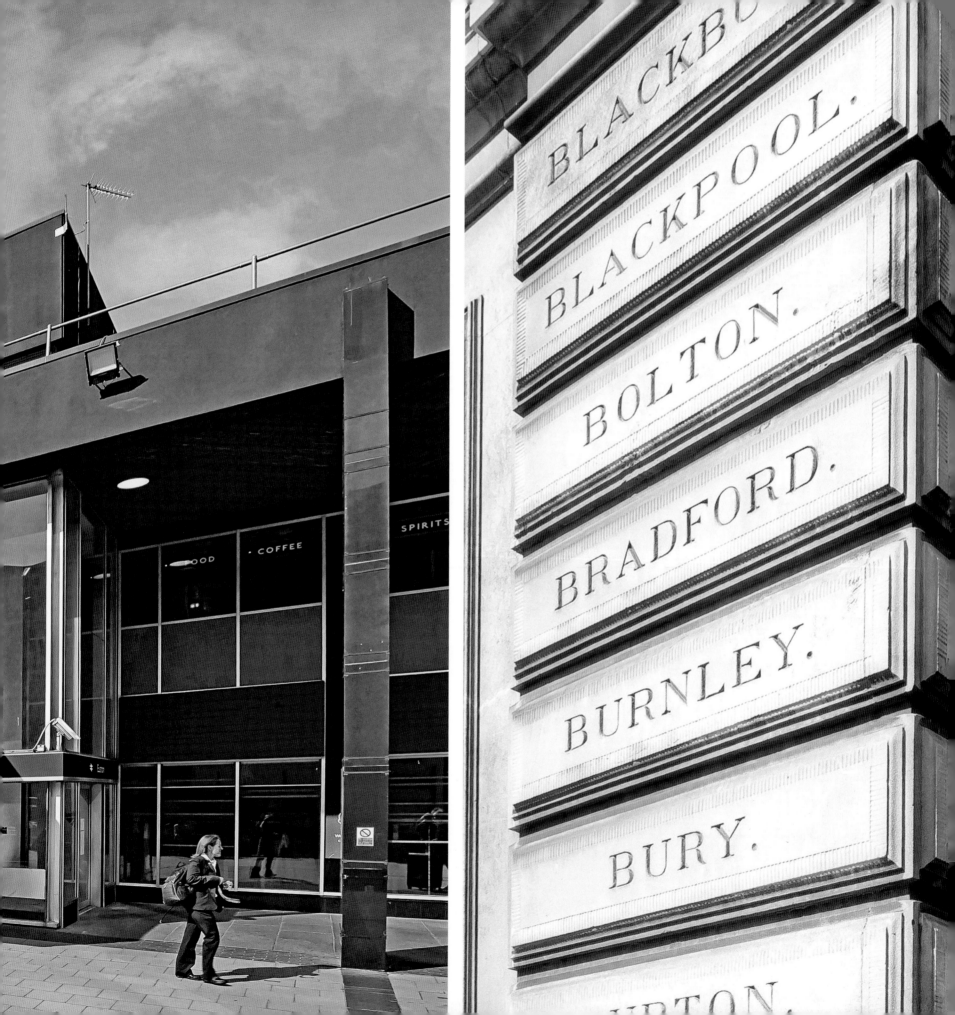

# FENCHURCH STREET

The façade of Fenchurch Street survives but I am not sure why. Its curved pediment expresses an arched train shed that no longer exists. Its 'row of Southend-on-Sea beach huts' awning is a frolicking caprice, all saucy Donald McGill postcards and deckchairs on the pier completely out of place in today's world (which may be a reason for keeping it) but it is not an adequate railway station. The monster building that rises above it, albeit stepped back and so relatively discreetly, is the real occupant of the site. It would have been better to have acknowledged the monster and taken the opportunity to create a pleasant and functional access to the trains, either with a completely modern frontage or – surely this was possible – taking more care and thought when incorporating the old. One limitation is that the front of the station was Grade II listed in 1972.

As it is, Fenchurch Street is an example of how not to update a station, the worst of all worlds. It is neither a restoration nor a proudly modern building. The ground floor entrance is claustrophobic, the first floor ticketing hall is dark and dank, the platform level treats train travel as something to get over and done with and the façade is nothing more than a sad remnant. This is dehumanising. The building above the station itself is largely anonymous while further down the tracks the enormous One America Square building straddles the railway lines and is anything but anonymous. This is in an Art Deco/Post Modern style and was built in 1988, and, surprisingly, designed by RHWL Architects, a firm quite capable of doing interesting work (such as Sheffield Crucible Theatre in 1971, and very recently St Pancras!) The problem probably lies in its size: 226,000 sq ft of offices. It is very much a building of the late 1980s.

However, the cavalry is on its way! The buildings can't be removed, of course, but a recently submitted planning application may rescue the station. Weston Williamson Architects, a firm that has been, and is, involved in upgrading many of London's termini (Waterloo, Paddington Elizabeth Line and more) proposes that, while retaining the frontage, other changes would take place. The ticketing area would be reconfigured, some of the retail space removed (an example that needs to be followed in other stations) or reconfigured, decorative finishes updated and, most importantly, the long-ignored windows opened up. This would allow previously banished light and views into the building. Weston Williamson describe their project as a 'retail upgrade' but it is more than that. The planning application suggests designers who want to respect both the historic building and the train user. I hope it happens.

The eleven tall windows of the first floor are set within bays of pale brick, with five sets of double doors below and have a pleasing rhythm which, to my mind, is disrupted by the zig-zag awning (a later replacement for the original, flat awning, which collapsed).

There is a pleasant little square in front of the station with an optimistic sign saying 'Arcadia', but perhaps the best thing about the station is its location, slap-bang in the oldest part of London, with the Tower of London to the south, Whitechapel to the east and with remnants of the city walls still standing in places. The ancient street pattern is revealed by the street names of Savage Gardens, Muscovy Street, Seething Lane, Pepys Street and Crutched Friars. There is a slightly labyrinthine approach to the station on foot from Tower Hill District line (there is no Underground link within the station) and Bank, Central line, is a fairish walk away.

Fenchurch Street was the first terminus within the City of London, but as the name of the original company suggests – the Commercial Railway – the line was built for goods traffic to and from the London docks. Renamed the London & Blackwall Railway, approval for the station was granted in 1839 and by 1840 a single track, cable traction service ran on a viaduct – the reason the platforms are on the first floor level. The cable haulage system, with a stationary engine pulling cars on the cable, like a ski lift, was one of the earliest forms of rail transportation. By 1849 the track had been relayed at standard gauge and steam traction introduced.

The London & Blackwall Railway operated the line from 1840 until it was leased by the Great Eastern Railway in 1866 and, until Liverpool Street opened in 1874-75, was the GER's terminus for suburban traffic. The London, Tilbury and Southend Railway also had a presence at the station.

The station was rebuilt and enlarged with the present day façade in 1854, to a design by George Berkley who had worked in the office of Robert Stephenson before establishing his own firm in 1849. As well as working in Britain, Berkley was involved in projects around the world, from South Africa to South America to India – not least the Great Indian Peninsular Railway.

The station was enlarged again in 1935 to accommodate longer trains in order to increase capacity, as a result of which bridges over the streets below needed to be strengthened. This made the Crosswall entrance an unexpected portal in the massive brickwork.

Although the building always had gloomy booking halls, photographs of the train shed make it look spacious and relatively light filled. The stairs up to the platforms look positively grand.

The area was named Crutched Friars after a Roman Catholic order that settled there in 1249 but was forced out in 1538 by the Dissolution of the Monasteries. The monks are now best remembered by the name of the local pub.

# KING'S CROSS

King's Cross seems so much more 'modern' than St Pancras that it is hard to believe that it was actually completed 16 years earlier. Great Northern Railway services ran to a temporary station in 1850 and the permanent structure, designed by Lewis Cubitt (working with William Cubitt, who had been chief engineer for the Great Exhibition Hall, and Joseph Cubitt) followed in 1852. With its pared-back façade unapologetically acknowledging the two sheds behind it and, unusually, not hidden behind a domineering hotel, the façade has more than stood the test of time. If it weren't for the anomalous, Italianate clock tower, the station could easily be imagined in some chilly Nordic country, such is its Lutheran austerity. *The Builder* in 1851 stated that the architect 'did not seek flamboyance, ostentation or effect' but sought only to express 'the fitness of the structure for its purpose'. Is this the start of 'modern' architecture?

The Great Northern Railway was incorporated in 1846 and was conceived, primarily, as a conduit for carrying coal from the coalfields of Yorkshire, Derbyshire and Nottinghamshire into London. The GNR had extended itself financially in purchasing land and in amalgamating with other rail companies to establish the route, but this may have been a blessing in disguise. Cubitt's design was simple and, certainly by comparison with Euston, cheap. No expense was wasted on anything. The fundamentals of the structure were given primacy and it is this rigour that makes the station so appealing to the modern eye. The shed ran 800ft in length. The original twin arches, each 105ft wide, were constructed using laminated timber – as had been the arches of Joseph Paxton's Great Conservatory at Chatsworth, its structural forerunner. This proved to be an unfortunate cost-saving attempt and they had to be replaced with iron in 1869.

Despite the very apparent need, a significant update had to wait until 2012 when the new forecourt building, set to the west of the original, was opened. By 2013 the Victorian frontage had been restored and the below ground functions greatly improved, with new Underground ticketing arrangements and new connecting passageways to facilitate changing lines.

The robust steel tracery of the self-supporting roof of the Western Concourse (by John McAslan+Partners architects with Arup) eschews any air-rights ambitions. It creates an elevating space which manages to pay tribute to both the engineering functionality of the King's Cross and St Pancras sheds and to the Gothic Revival of the St Pancras hotel. This can best be described as glorious. The mezzanine sales floor is an integral part of the design and it slithers snake-like, and suitably clad in mosaic tiles, through the building, but I would rather it wasn't there. It seems an intruder in the otherwise ethereal space (although it functions as part of the circulation of the station as well as being, it has to be said, a pleasant place to refresh oneself).

The developers of the greater King's Cross area, Argent St George, and the landowners, London and Continental Railways and Excel, wanted to 'recognise, celebrate' and, in so far as possible, preserve the industrial heritage of the site. By most measures they have succeeded. The entire development has certainly been highly praised.

The University of the Arts now occupies the old Granary building and the Coal Drops Yard is now 'high end retailing' with one of Thomas Heatherwick's characteristically imaginative and ambitious designs. The almost-but-not-quite Mobius strip of the roof (which ends up being a bit 'so what?') and the delightful open spaces, especially close to the Regent's Canal, are popular summer haunts. There is still, however, a lot of unaffordable (and probably 'investment') property which will surely further distort the housing market.

The fact that Camden council has always been notable for its bold architectural plans to provide good quality housing for its residents and its encouragement of urban regeneration, suggests that its involvement in the King's Cross scheme will have been beneficial. Let's hope so. When the King's Cross development was originally mooted, I imagined it being the site of a mega transport hub, uniting King's Cross with St Pancras while, at least, demoting Euston if not completely dispensing with it by commandeering its lines to the north. This would have created a nexus for seamless travel from Scotland and the north of England to France and the rest of Europe. Having more railway and less housing would have been a hard sell.

Holding back some of the site to allow for possible future travel infrastructure would have been an even harder sell. On the basis of the supermarket retailing acronym, WIGIG (When It's Gone It's Gone) I fear for 'What's Gone', namely the potential. That is the ability to respond to new transport needs, with new technology, from a central location in London.

# LIVERPOOL STREET

In the frenzied years of terminus building in the middle of the 19th century, the battle fought over access to the City of London was one of the more convoluted and protracted. The North London Railway (NLR), working with the London and North Western Railway, opened a high level station at Broad Street in 1865. Although the railway companies that eventually became the NLR had originally been conceived as goods lines, by the time the NLR was formed (1853) it had become apparent that passenger traffic would play an increasingly important role in the prosperity of the company.

A series of mergers in 1862 had made the Great Eastern Railway (GER) its chief rival, but, in the short term at least, it was less successful. One of the constituent companies, the Eastern Counties Railway, had managed to inch closer and closer to the City, first opening a station in Mile End in 1839 and then a more permanent station in Shoreditch in 1840. This, however, was still too far from the City and in an area of desperate poverty. This made using the station a gauntlet run between pickpockets, robbers, child snatchers and prostitutes. In 1846 it was renamed Bishopsgate 'probably in the hope that it might be thought nearer the City than it was' (Alan A. Jackson, *London's Termini*) and perhaps more salubrious. That didn't work, so the station remained in use for many years. Negotiations with the NLR to use Broad Street foundered and in 1864 Parliament approved a station at Liverpool Street.

The duplication of facilities at Liverpool Street and Broad Street made them an obvious target for redevelopment in the late 20th century. The fact that Liverpool Street station wasn't razed is a tribute to public opposition, the Railway Heritage Trust, SAVE Britain's Heritage and to a developer prepared to honour the original design. This was due also to the team of BR architects, led by Nick Derbyshire, which designed the new station in the 1980s. Broad Street had to be sacrificed and is now the site of the whopping – 32 acre (13ha) – Broadgate retail and office city-within-a-city.

Whether the 1975 British Rail plans for demolishing both stations and creating a twenty two platform station below ground level with offices above would have been better is debatable – but it is highly unlikely. The Liverpool Street that survives is hugely successful in most ways.

Air rights were sacrificed over some of the tracks on the east side to finance what was the virtual rebuilding of the entire station, but the architects were at pains to replicate the original design by the GER's chief engineer, Edward Wilson, working with his nephew John Wilson. Perhaps more significantly, this also involved the work of the GER architect William Ashbee, who was later responsible for the station at Norwich. The attention to detail in the renovation went all the way down to the acanthus capitals on the forest of columns. Parts were rebuilt, parts are new (including the whole eastern shed), but were brought together in such a way that you would not know the difference between them. Cultural historian Steven Parissien judges it to be 'the only air-rights scheme which displayed any imagination or sympathy for the historic station'.

The Great Eastern Hotel in Liverpool Street itself (now the Andaz) defines the southern and eastern boundaries of the station and, despite being built in two stages and in two different styles, makes a very positive contribution to the street and to the station. The same cannot be said of the air-rights building on Broadgate. Nor of the lighting at the south entrance, nor the rain canopies at both entrances, each of which feel dated and ungainly. A statue remembering the Kinder Transports of the 1930s is admirable in spirit but not entirely successful in its placement.

A technical decision made by the Great Eastern Railway had brought the trains in at just below street level, to create a junction with the Metropolitan Railway. This meant that the present concourse is set in an amphitheatre. It makes one's arrival an event: at the street entrances to the station, the traveller has the option to pause for a moment to look down onto the concourse rather than being thrust directly into the scrum.

By all accounts, the rebuilding simplified what had been a Piranesian mishmash of confusion but, more than at any other station, the 'retail offering' is infuriatingly intrusive. To say the least it is a crime perpetrated on the train shed. The extruded igloo of commercial units that has been squeezed out across the platforms ruins the sightlines and destroys the drama of the receding arches and the snaking carriages. They are however a useful source of revenue for the railway and provide a service of benefit to the passengers. To get an idea of what you could be looking at, stay on the higher level, dodge down the alley beside M&S, skirt past the tanning salon and discover the tropical house of exotic palms that the many columns resemble. Each column has its own acanthus crown from which cast iron ribs with perforated spandrels fan out.

The Great Eastern Hotel was designed by Charles Barry Jnr and Edward Middleton Barry, sons of Charles 'Houses of Parliament' Barry and opened in 1884. An annexe by Robert William Edis, who also designed Marylebone's Great Central Hotel, was added in 1901 and the lavish interior included Hamilton Hall, which was once used as a ballroom but is now – cruel fate – a thriving Wetherspoons pub. The Grecian room boasts a gilded zodiac ceiling, twelve types of marble, heavy mahogany doors and 'original' leather and gold thrones. I'm not sure that there is an accepted description for the style but I'm pretty sure it's not 'Grecian'. In 2000 Manser Architects undertook a substantial renovation of the hotel, incorporating a monumental atrium (but thankfully leaving the Temples alone).

# LONDON BRIDGE

If you are going to build a vertical money ghetto it might as well be a breath-taking, beautiful column of cash like The Shard, Renzo Piano's stunning tower, and if it helps to finance the rebuilding of an important station like (the previously loathed) London Bridge then maybe it can be justified, at least on its own terms. The Shard is, unlike so many other towers built or planned for London, a fabulous addition to the skyline. The station, by Grimshaw, makes the very most of the sometimes limited vocabulary of modern railway station concourse design. London Bridge is impressively and refreshingly spacious and functional. Christian Wolmar (*Cathedrals of Steam*), while acknowledging its strengths, still describes it as 'a rather messy amalgam of two stations'.

The new concourse is the size of Wembley football pitch and the structural elements are suitably monumental. Grimshaw does not shy away from grandiose statements. The individual is – quite rightly – dwarfed by the scale, but the immensity isn't used to diminish the spirit of the individual but to elevate it. The way daylight is harnessed and manipulated is a heartening example of Le Corbusier's dictum that architecture is the play of masses brought together in light. The fact that the ground floor level is a cascade of escalators does not diminish this. Or the fact that the main line trains on the upper level seem like a prosaic afterthought in comparison to the architecture.

All fifteen platforms are linked by the low level concourse but London Bridge is more a 'multi-modal transport hub' than a simple railway station. The new station was opened in 2018 and as well as being a main line station for South Eastern, Southern and Thameslink, it is also served by London Underground's Northern and Jubilee lines. It is designed to cope with more than 90 million passengers a year.

Even the platforms – so often treated as an afterthought – have been carefully considered. The sinuously curved canopies that follow the flow of the tracks are described by the architects, rather sweetly, as 'eyebrows'. These are a delight.

Many of the old, brick-built elements of the previous station, both internally and externally, have been incorporated into the new design, many having to be rebuilt. Conservation architects Donald Insall Associates were brought in to the project to ensure accurate and sympathetic reconstruction. Insall describes the 'polychromatic (brick) frontages', designed by John Henry Driver, as 'unique' and they have been carefully restored. The brickwork of the subterranean stairways and tunnels makes for an especially atmospheric experience, notably the Western Arcade that links the National Rail station to the Underground. The arches are stylishly – and appropriately for a change – occupied by shops.

Pascall+Watson, another design practice involved in a number of station updates, such as King's Cross and Blackfriars, worked with Renzo Piano Building Workshop to create the link between The Shard and the mainline station, incorporating bus and taxi services around a light-filled piazza.

London Bridge was the first passenger terminus built in London (beating Euston by a number of months) but the original station had no train shed and no buildings of note. In 1831, approval was given to build three and a half miles of track over a brick viaduct of 878 arches between Greenwich and Tooley Street, at London Bridge. These remain the longest set of arches in Britain and it is only right that these arches should be celebrated where they meet the modern station.

In 1836 the London & Greenwich Railway opened the first section, becoming both the first passenger and the first steam railway in London, and two years later the line was completed. There followed a proliferation of train companies wanting to use the line and by 1844 a Joint Station was built for the use of four different companies: the London & Greenwich, the London & Croydon, the South Eastern Railway and the London & Brighton Railway. This sharing arrangement worked less and less harmoniously. In 1850 the SER built a wall down the middle of the station, with its own terminus on the northern side.

The next major event in the life of London Bridge station was the removal of the wall between the two stations in 1928. This followed the Grouping of 1923, an attempt by government to rationalise and consolidate the rail network. All the companies serving London Bridge, plus others, became part of the Southern Railway.

It was, however, always a hugely well-used station (if not a popular one). By the 1900s there were twenty-one platforms (fifteen terminal ones and six through lines) and electrification of the lines only increased capacity.

After all that, Grimshaw's station seems like a masterwork of rationalisation.

Southwark has been in the grip of regeneration for some time and I imagine the developers of The Shard will hope this continue apace. The occupants of the chauffeur-driven Rolls-Royces heading for Shangri-La (the hotel) probably won't leave their fortress for an evening stroll – but if this gentrification could liberate some of the waterfront it might be worthwhile. Too many large buildings dipping their toes in the river prevent any sort of spacious promenade, however, so maybe better access to the pier for Transport for London's River Bus service is the most that can be wished for at the moment.

# MARYLEBONE

Last of the London termini to be built (1899), Marylebone should have been the grandest. It certainly came from a mind fizzing with ideas and ambition. Sir Edward Watkin (1819-1901) dreamed of linking Britain's industrial cities of the north to the Continent by running a new rail line into London right down the spine of England. His plan was to create a Great Central Railway (GCR) that linked the existing Manchester, Sheffield & Lincolnshire Railway (of which he became chairman in 1864) to London, and then on to continental Europe. This would run via the Metropolitan Railway (of which he became chairman in 1872) and the South Eastern Railway (chairman from 1866) and a proposed Channel tunnel to France (chairman of that company too, obviously). In fact, he became a director of no fewer than nine railway companies, and his aspirations were not limited by geography; he was involved in schemes in Canada, the USA, India, Africa and Greece. He was ahead of his time.

The Metropolitan Railway was the world's first underground railway. Its first stage opened in 1863 and ran from Paddington to Farringdon Street via King's Cross. It also ran over-ground, reaching as far out from London as Aylesbury by 1892. This made it both the ideal route into the city but also the vital link for the GCR's ambitions of onward travel.

Baker Street station near the south-western corner of Regent's Park, was on the Metropolitan line and Watkin had hoped to terminate the intercity line there. However, the realities of topography and construction meant that it could not be upgraded to take heavy trains. As a result, 51 acres of largely slum dwellings were purchased slightly further west at Marylebone and became the site for the terminus. 2,690 of the displaced persons were rehoused in Wharncliffe Dwellings, blocks of flats built by the GCR. Although permission was granted for a connection between Marylebone and the Metropolitan Railway by a parliamentary Act in 1893, the option was never taken up due to the cost involved and opposition on many fronts.

Despite the best efforts of the Marylebone Cricket Club, based at Lord's ground in St. John's Wood, the line was eventually built but the time and expense of finally reaching its destination meant that the GCR was financially impoverished. It had also lost its visionary chairman who resigned after suffering a stroke in 1894.

The station building itself is the poor relation of London termini. Its design was entrusted to H.W. Braddock, a company engineer, but its 'quaintly frayed around the edges' feeling appeals to me. 'Provincial' is the word that has been used by more than one writer to patronisingly describe Marylebone, but maybe that is its charm. A trio of arches faced with terracotta the colour of blancmange gone bad marks the main entrance to the concourse from the street while a porte cochere of fine cast iron columns supporting a glazed roof lightly dappled with green mould links the station to the hotel. The train shed, without being special, is light and airy and the red-painted columns give the platforms a zing. The roof itself is ridged parallel to the frontage and supported on girders.

There are things I don't like about it – the trek to the more distant platforms resembles a Great Migration at rush hour – and there are things I loathe about it – the commercial intrusions are particularly substantial and unpleasant, and the Gents' toilet is really quite nasty – but nothing that couldn't be bulldozed.

Watkin's intercontinental dreams came to nothing and the GCR could never compete adequately with the older companies running to the North. By the 1920s, commuter travel to south Buckinghamshire was becoming more and more important. British Rail persevered with services to Sheffield, Bradford and Manchester but all mainline services north of Aylesbury ended in 1966.

I am saddened that you can no longer travel from Marylebone to Sheffield via Rugby, Leicester and Nottingham. There may have been a case for closing the GCR line in part, but if only the physical route had been preserved the debate about the path of HS2 might have been very different.

Today, most of Marylebone's destinations are within the commuter sprawl of Metroland, but there is also a substantial service to Bicester, Banbury, Leamington Spa and Birmingham Moor Street, with some services to Oxford. Together, these keep Marylebone's six platforms busy.

The Great Central Hotel – now the Landmark London – is a vast and imposing pile of terracotta and brick. It would have been a suitably grand announcement of the Great Central Railway's arrival in London, were it not for the GCR running out of cash. The hotel had to be financed by Sir Blundell Maple, the furniture magnate. It was designed by Col. R.W. Edis (who was responsible for the addition to the Great Eastern Hotel at Liverpool Street) and Sir John Betjeman was particularly fond of it.

After its early glory days, the hotel went into some decline but had a fascinating history, including being the location for a 'Welcome back from prison' celebration for Emmeline Pankhurst in 1908 and the base for MI9, a Second World War secret intelligence unit. For a while it was the headquarters of British Rail and not so lovingly known as 'the Kremlin'. Restored to some elegance recently it has a missile silo-sized atrium and a five-star rating from *Time Out* magazine.

# PADDINGTON

The Paddington of 1854 is one of the Goliaths of London stations and it has, thankfully, been respectfully updated. The driving force behind the station, and the Great Western Railway that the terminus served, was the incomparable Isambard Kingdom Brunel. He was born in 1806 and died tragically young for a man of his talents, aged 53 in 1859. He is rightly regarded as a Titan of the early Victorian era. A prolific and versatile engineering genius, he built railways, bridges, docks, tunnels and transatlantic steamships. None of his projects lacked ambition. His life was devoted to and consumed by engineering. Together with St Pancras and King's Cross – the survivors of the truly magnificent arched train sheds of London – Paddington is built on an awe-inspiring scale.

A temporary station at Paddington opened in 1838, serving only an initial short route to Taplow. The train shed we now see was designed by Brunel, together with Matthew Digby Wyatt, who was assigned the job of detailing the structure. It was opened formally in 1854 as the London terminus of the Great Western Railway. Huge, mighty, imposing, impressive, the design and construction reference both Joseph Paxton's Great Exhibition building and mediaeval cathedral architecture. The main shed serves as the nave, the secondary, smaller, arches represent the aisles and the transverse elements the transepts. A fourth shed was added in the 20th century parallel to the original three. Wyatt's contribution should not be ignored: the wrought iron screens that terminate the arches and anticipate art nouveau are his, as are the quirky window bays at Platform 1, in a style that has had commentators describing them as Elizabethan, Venetian and Moorish.

The 1999 Grimshaw renovation is masterful. Embracing what they describe as the 'architecture of reduction' Grimshaw and his partners undertook to reveal the original shed and free it of the ad hoc additions of the intervening years. Perhaps the most telling intervention – and also the simplest – was to remove the main information display from its position across the platform ends and create a number of smaller, less visually obstructive boards positioned at right angles to the original and in alignment with the platforms.

This allows the eye to follow the path of the roof and take in the gargantuan scale of the building. Such a simple adjustment was completely transformative. Quite how enthusiastically it has been received by the travelling public emerging from the Underground, wanting only their platform number, is another matter.

A lot of the retail outlets have been contained within the area known as The Lawn, which was once the Station Master's garden (or a dismal overflow space for parcel storage and hotel deliveries, depending on which source you believe and how romantic your nature is). The usual visual pollution of competing shop signage is not overwhelming and does not detract from the majestic structure. Within The Lawn itself, airport aesthetic meets Marks & Spencer's aesthetic to create a polite, but bland area. Grimshaw's concept of a space to relax in and admire the views of the train shed from a number of levels seems to have been compromised, offering too much shopping and not enough sitting.

The Great Western Royal Hotel (now owned by Hilton) frontage says nothing about the marvel beyond. In fact, the hotel squeezes the approach to the concourse from Praed Street and makes it seem as if it is the station that has intruded onto the hotel's territory.

The approach is not without interest, though, provided you look up to take in the higher floors of P. G. Culverhouses's 'moderne' style GWR Offices (1933) (now known as Tournament House). Culverhouse also 'modernised' the interior of the hotel, much to most rail historians' dismay.

Its Louis XIV-ish facade is certainly an imposing street presence but its fantasy blend of Classical and French architecture (by Philip Hardwick, who also designed the Great Hall at Euston station) demonstrates the limits of Victorian acceptance of an engineering-based aesthetic. For four storeys the façade has a pleasing asperity, but the mansard roof goes a bit funny because it is punctured by too many bland windows, and the towers that bookend the Praed Street elevation are simply odd, overscaled and awkward. The hotel is notable for starting the tradition of fronting the railway sheds of London termini with large and luxurious hotels.

The Crossrail concept was as ambitious as any of the first railways and its engineering achievements are as great or perhaps even greater. A whole new Elizabeth Line station has been created on the Eastbourne Terrace side of the Brunel structure. A 120m long steel and glass canopy, 8m above ground level, fills the space with natural light. Weston Williamson, already involved in the Paddington Integrated Project, have designed something which would impress even Brunel.

The impressive soldier statue on platform 1 is The Great Western Railway War Memorial and was commissioned in 1920 to commemorate the employees of the Great Western Railway (GWR) who had died during the First World War. The bronze figure was created by the sculptor Charles Sargeant Jagger. Dressed in battle gear with greatcoat, the soldier is looking down, reading a letter from home. In complete contrast, a statue of Paddington Bear also stands on Platform 1, under the station clock, which was unveiled in February 2000.

The seated figure of Isambard Brunel at the station was unveiled in May 1982. It is one of two statues of Brunel commissioned by the Bristol & West Building Society. A standing figure of Brunel was unveiled in Bristol at the same time. Paddington's has been moved three times and is today located between Platforms 8 and 9, giving Brunel a good view across the main-line platforms.

For information please call
0800 197 1329

Paddington Station

# ST PANCRAS

The rebirth of St Pancras is a triumph but, I have to confess, the first time I saw the hotel – sometime in the late 1970s at its most desolate in a no-man's land between demolition and decay – I was very much of the opinion that it was the last word in ghastliness and did not deserve to survive. Luckily, I was not in a position to influence the debate at that time and John Betjeman and his fellow conservationists won the day. While modernist architects, engineers and planners could safely admire the great shed, the hotel roused stronger passions and exposed deeper divisions. The only excuse I have for my desire to see it razed was that faith in the new is infectious – and as much a part of the Victorians' makeup as of any of the architects of the International Style.

Neglected, reviled and threatened with oblivion, for many people the hotel stood as the manifestation of the battle between a sentimentalised view of the past and a dynamic vision of the future. It was the conflict between conservative and radical, style and function. The station went into decline when the London Midland & Scottish Railway company took over management from the Midland Railway in 1923 and concentrated its efforts on nearby Euston. The coming of British Railways in 1948 did not help. The hotel closed in the 1930s. BR tried to close and demolish the station more than once but Betjeman and his cohort managed to get both the station and hotel listed just days before demolition was due to begin in 1967. It is today faithfully restored.

The trainshed was always admired. Who could not be impressed by it? Who could not be awed by it? In comparison with the hotel building, the shed was lean, taut and ascetic: structure expressed in the most disciplined of ways. It does have decorative features, but usually no more than the name of the company that manufactured the ironwork (Butterley for example), cast into the metal. Forgivable pride. It is a marvel, and in its day was the largest enclosed structure in the world. It is huge: 689 feet long, while the single span design covers the 243ft width at 100ft high.

An engineer, not an architect, designed it. William Henry Barlow was the consulting engineer for the Midland Railway and he was responsible both for bringing the tracks the 50 miles from Bedford into London and locating the terminus. He had worked with Joseph Paxton on the Great Exhibition Hall of 1851 and the debt owed to Paxton in the audacious sweep of the arched roof is evident. A single span was not the original conception; a twin span design was considered but discarded because Barlow had faith in the structural integrity of the single-span. The Midland Railway saw the potential of the uncluttered platform area and the basement below.

The Midland Railway – headquartered in Derby – had arrived in London in 1858, but only by using Great Northern Railway tracks for the final 32 mile leg from Hitchin. It was an unsustainable relationship and in 1862 the Midland made the decision to create its own route. This involved weaving the tracks under the North London Railway and over the Regent's Canal, meaning the platform level would be 20ft above the Euston Road and above the already existing King's Cross. This created a wonderful opportunity for capacious below-track cellaring for the barrels of Burton Beer that the railway was going to transport from Burton-upon-Trent on the Staffordshire-Derbyshire border to the ever-growing market of London. The barrels themselves became the unit of measurement for the spacing of the 850 cast iron pillars that were to support the platform level, and the decision to use a single-span roof was made in no small part to obviate the need for the substantial, large-diameter additional columns and their expensive foundations that a double span roof would require. The station opened in 1868.

The serendipitous relationship of Burton beer and St Pancras bore fruit again in the renovation of the station: the undercroft became one of the key elements in the 2001 redevelopment plan. Opening it up on either side of the tracks allowed an extraordinary amount of commercial space to be included in the design, which sensitively incorporated the columns and arches, while allowing the Eurostar platforms to remain uncluttered, and natural light to penetrate to the lower level. It was the opening of the Channel Tunnel in 1994 and the decision to make St Pancras the terminal for HS1 (the Eurostar line) that gave the momentum to its glorious restoration.

The neat, sleek, functional extension – carried out to a design concept by Foster and Partners and needed to accommodate both the Eurostar trains and domestic rail services – added 200m to the overall length of the station. The junction between old and new received some criticism but, to my mind, it is visually successful and very definitely functionally successful. It creates two new entrance points, one on Midland Road – the Euston side – and the other on Pancras Road facing the West Concourse of King's Cross, making the greater King's Cross area feel integrated with both stations.

The statue of Sir John Betjeman is a deserved tribute (and an appropriate size). The statue of an anonymous couple embracing – The Meeting Place – is very big (30ft tall) and the best thing about it is the relief frieze that encircles the base, pictured on the fifth spread of this chapter. It is considered to be one of the world's most romantic spots, according to a *Lonely Planet* poll.

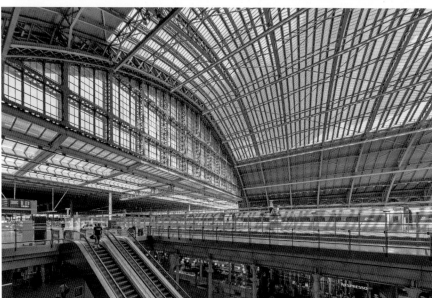

↑ Underground ⊖
← Arrivals Arrivées
↑ Way out
♿ 🚻 Toilets

# VICTORIA

Victoria Station was the result of competing rail companies vying for ascendency. The ultimate prize was a station north of the river and close to the City of Westminster and the West End. It was divided into the Chatham and the Brighton sides.

By 1858 the Victoria Station and Pimlico Railway (VS&PR) had been set up as a joint venture by four rail companies to bridge the Thames and create a new station between Pimlico, Belgravia and Westminster. After a period where shifting alliances and the ensuing plethora of company names muddied the waters, the eventual duel became one between two train companies: the London, Brighton & South Coast Railway (LB&SCR) and the London Chatham & Dover Railway (LC&DR). John Fowler, one of the genius-engineers of the age, built Grosvenor Bridge, the first railway bridge to span the Thames in central London. This was for the VS&PR company but the rivalry between the LC&DR and the LB&SCR then asserted itself. The Brighton company won the race to open its side of Victoria station in 1860. It was designed by Robert Jacomb Hood; it stands on the western "Buckingham Palace Road" side of the present terminus, now platforms 9-17. The Chatham company completed its adjoining train shed designed by Fowler on the eastern Wilton Road side, platforms 1-8 in 1862.

This shed is described by Historic England as 'one of the lightest and most elegant of the major station roofs from this period' while Hood's creation was considered prosaic in comparison. It is unfortunate that commercial rivalry prevented Fowler from taking overall charge of the entire structure. His arches are almost alarmingly delicate, a light filigree that belies their strength. What a shame that the view down the platforms is now truncated by a big black glass box.

The LB&SCR completely rebuilt their side of the station between 1898 and 1908, doubling the acreage from 8.5 to 16, and replacing the original ridge and furrow roof with louvred ridge roofs running parallel with the tracks. In 1907 Grosvenor Bridge was widened to 178ft to take the extra traffic and, as Alan A. Jackson notes in *London's Termini*, was 'in effect, three separate bridges' to accommodate the competing companies. The bridge had to be completely rebuilt in 1967.

Theoretically at least, the Brighton and Chatham companies shared the concourse but they were so hostile to each other that the dividing wall between the two stations was only breached in 1924. The wall is still traceable, although now pierced in a number of places, and largely hidden by retail outlets. I would rather see the wall.

Neither company 'bothered to add any architectural embellishment to the joint frontage' for the next forty years, but the grandest of grand hotels, the Grosvenor, was built independently in 1861. According to one commentator, this gave the area 'its only real architectural presence in the nineteenth century' and described by another as 'the greatest hotel London had yet seen'. It's certainly palatial and would not be out of place on the seafront at Cannes.

The LB&SCR bought the Grosvenor in 1899 and built a new wing across the station entrance, finally creating an imposing entrance, albeit in a style described as 'rather pompous .. Edwardian baroque'. I like it, perhaps because it is pompous, with its mansard roofs, tall chimneys, red brick and Portland stone facade, and, not least, its 'illuminated clock flanked by recumbent figures' (Alan A Jackson again). Unfortunately, the frontage is dominated, if not overwhelmed, by the functional but gargantuan and inelegant awning that shelters travellers from the rain. I would also imagine that it makes them feel miserable for reasons that they can't quite put their fingers on.

The Chatham responded – fabulously – in 1910 with an extravagant Portland stone fantasy of mermaid caryatids, rusticated pilasters, pediments both broken and not, wreaths and more than one decorated cartouche, in what looks to me like a *Mitteleuropa* fever dream. This was all arranged around the 'Royal entrance' to the station, an archway flanked by 'paired Roman Doric columns ... with narrow arched niches in between the columns'. These lead to the 'Royal waiting rooms', where foreign royalty visiting from abroad could be welcomed (or sent packing).

The District Railway (later to become the District and Circle lines) opened a station immediately north of the terminus in 1868, the Victoria line following in 1969/71.

Nowadays a polite entrance to the Tube – the cleanest and simplest of designs – stands, through no fault of its own, far too close to the Disney-esque façade. I wonder if it could have been smaller? Or completely transparent? Or circular? Or not there at all? I have no answer, but it does detract from the frontage. As does the visitor centre and the backside of Burger King, an ironic V-sign to the pompous aspirations of the Ruritanian tsars and kaisers of old.

Victoria has always been the London main line station for Gatwick Airport, which started operating in 1958 and is a significant part of its business.  The railway station and the adjoining bus station set out to make Victoria a transport hub and in 1962 British United Airways opened a terminal within the station, a steel and glass structure set on stilts above the old cab road between platforms 15 and 18, designed by Clive Pascall.

The area immediately in front of the station, which used to be ghastly, has been tidied up and opposite the station is an outcrop of new towers, such as the Nova Victoria, which will not be to everybody's taste. It was awarded the 2017 Carbuncle Cup by Building Design magazine for the UK's ugliest building.

# WATERLOO

While Paris is littered with railway stations named in honour of Napoleonic victories in battle, British station nomenclature has been less militaristic. Waterloo station is the exception – although it is only indirectly one in the eye for the French. Strictly speaking, the station takes its name from the bridge (which was, however, named to celebrate Napoleon's defeat). The main architectural feature of its exterior is the Memorial Arch of 1922 which was built to honour the railway employees who died in the First World War. It is, however, generally known as the Victory Arch.

Waterloo is big and it has long been London's busiest station (94 million passengers in 2018/19, but it shouldn't even exist as a major terminus. The London & South Western Railway (L&SWR) Company's plan had been to run their line across or under the river to get closer to the lucrative markets of the City and the West End, using Waterloo only as a junction stop on the way. The failure of these plans meant that, although the opening date of Waterloo station is accepted as 1848, the station proper only took shape over a period of three decades at the beginning of the 20th century. Permission was granted in 1900 and site clearance began; in 1909 building work began, only to be interrupted by the First World War. The rebuilt and much enlarged station was opened officially by HM Queen Mary on 21 March 1922.

The roof of the shed is not a great arched structure, so it doesn't have the drama of other stations, but it is high and the way the roof lines run at right angles from the main building over the concourse but switch orientation over the platforms is interesting. Under the roof is an enormous clock, visible from all parts of the concourse.

The station does not work well in its relationship to its immediate neighbourhood. Main line tracks that did eventually make it across the river, running to Charing Cross, cut their way directly in front of Waterloo, and the horrible road system does the same. Together, these destroy any chance Waterloo might have had to relate constructively with its vicinity.

Getting to the Victory Arch on foot seems like a triumph in itself and it is even harder to find the distance necessary to visually enjoy it than at the other London stations. Instead, it suddenly presents itself among a hugger-mugger of distractions. These, however, are picturesque. The blue lattice steel work of a railway bridge, the great sweep of the tracks toward Charing Cross, and the slab-like porte cochere that shelters bus passengers and taxi users. These are slung with guano-filled anti-pigeon nets, threatening to sunder and shower their contents over any unfortunate enough to be beneath them at the time. The sheer materiality of the stonework counterpoints the chaos around it. As an example of ugly-beauty Waterloo scores highly.

When you get inside this is replaced by the chaotic beauty of the older part of the trainshed roof. A chatter of struts and girders, it is impossible to find visual peace looking at it. It works better than a cup of coffee.

The one-time Eurostar addition to the older building, however, is blissful, a throwback to the leaping arches of the 'cathedrals of steam', and its sinuous caterpillar curve is a joy. The blue tubular supports may not be quite as elegant, say, as the ribbed arches of Paddington, but the modular building system that they are part of is genius. The 'fish scales' of overlapping glass sheets and the universal component structure that copes with the curved, asymmetric geometries are pure engineering heaven and a nod to Joseph Paxton. The International Terminal Waterloo (Grimshaw) opened in 1994 and I remember the excitement I felt when Eurostar first ran. It seemed like a declaration that the Little England thinking of prejudiced, bigoted small-mindedness would be displaced by the opening of a wider horizon and that Folkestone wasn't the end of the line, Paris was the beginning. Waterloo was a world-beating design, symbolising a new, technologically confident Britain. The French President, François Mitterrand, was at the other end of the tunnel to greet HM The Queen when she made her trip. *Entente tres cordiale.*

Oh well, that dream's over.

In 2007 European services were moved to what is now London St Pancras International and, after many years of being mothballed, the Eurostar platform has been given a purpose again. A mundane purpose, perhaps, serving local lines, but it is still beautiful. Lucky commuters, is what I say.

The retail mezzanine is as well done as I suspect it could be and it allows you to see close-up the decorative stonework that you would never notice from ground level – the L&SWR arms, garlanded with laurels; the high-relief carvings of named destinations; a leaded window design celebrating the original train company – and it provided an eyrie for me to sit, drink coffee and observe the travellers milling around below. If, that is, I could pull my eyes away from the gargantuan advertising screens.

To see the original site of Waterloo Junction, follow the signs to Waterloo East (if you can find them) and use the covered pedestrian bridge – a grubby cross between '*2001: A Space Odyssey*' and a public urinal – over Waterloo Road which will drop you down onto the platforms of Waterloo East.

If you exit the station on this side, the terraced houses of the Roupell Street Conservation Area are a trip back in time to the 1830s.

# Bibliography

There are many detailed accounts of the history of the railways and of the London termini, some of which are listed below. Our book tries to set the scene and encourage further exploration.

*Cathedrals of Steam* by Christian Wolmar, Atlantic Books, 2020. A true enthusiast's book that manages to read like a novel. The book's subtitle – How London's *Great Stations Were Built And How They Transformed the City* – shows the scope of the work and why it is not just for rail buffs.

*Britain's 100 Best Railway Stations* by Simon Jenkins, Penguin Books, 2021. The closest we have to a modern day Betjeman. Anything Jenkins writes is worth reading.

*The English Railway Station* by Steven Parissien, Historic England, 2014. Like Jenkins, Parissien is another prolific historian with an interest in the railways. Photographs from the English Heritage archive are fascinating.

*London's Historic Railway Stations* by Sir John Betjeman, Capital Transport, 2002. This book by the great advocate for preserving Britain's architectural history has the added advantage of fine, atmospheric photographs by John Gay to accompany Betjeman's engaging text.

*Discovering London Railway Stations* by Oliver Green, Shire Books, 2010. A succinct, easily readable and hugely informative work.

*The Age of Capital 1848 – 1875* by Eric Hobsbawm, Abacus Books, 1988. A compendious history of the time and a vital work for putting the railways into their context. Its breadth and depth are remarkable.

The website for University College London's Centre for the Study of the Legacies of British Slavery makes for chastening reading: www.ucl.ac.uk

Investigating the websites of any of the contemporary architects mentioned in this book will fill you with optimism. The talent is extraordinary.

For those interested in disappearing down rabbit holes of unexpected information, the website www.ianVisits.co.uk keeps a journalistic eye on the most up to date London rail transport news.